BIG BOOK OF Cloze

Extreme (1) sports include excitement, skills and danger with **several** (2) activities below ground, in the air and on the water.

To reach space the **rockets** (5) need to make the spacecraft attain the speed of **eight** (6) kilometres per second.

Salt eventually kills the plants

Salty water

Watertable rises

Salinity is slow and silent; it may be **years** (25) before farmers **notice** (26) that their trees are dying.

Big Book of Cloze
Upper

Published by Prim-Ed Publishing® 2012
Copyright© R.I.C. Publications® 2012
ISBN 978-1-84654-552-8

PR–9232

Additional titles available in this series:
Big Book of Cloze – *Lower*
Big Book of Cloze – *Middle*
Big Book of Cloze – *Upper*

Internet websites
In some cases, websites or specific URLs may be recommended. While these are checked and rechecked at the time of publication, the publisher has no control over any subsequent changes which may be made to webpages. It is *strongly* recommended that the class teacher checks *all* URLs before allowing pupils to access them.

View all pages online

Website: http://www.prim-ed.com

Foreword

The **Big Book of Cloze – Upper** is a compilation of great cloze activities from a range of Cloze series, published over the years, which have proven to be successful. Republished in a contemporary format, this series represents the best of great cloze activities for the classroom. Activities have been taken from three previous series: (i) *Cloze in on Language*, (ii) *Contemporary Cloze* and (iii) *Cloze Encounters*.

Books in this series include: *Big Book of Cloze – Lower*
Big Book of Cloze – Middle
Big Book of Cloze – Upper

Contents

Curriculum Links

Country	Subject	Level	Objectives
England	English	Years 5 and 6	• read a range of books • understand what they read by building on the skills developed in Years 3 and 4
Northern Ireland	Language and literacy	KS 2	• read and understand a range of texts • justify their responses logically • use a range of cross-checking strategies to read unfamiliar words in texts • use a variety of reading skills
Republic of Ireland	English	5th/6th Class	• engage with an increasing range of text • read widely as an independent reader from a more challenging range of reading material • use comprehension skills
Scotland	Literacy and English	Second	• develop knowledge of context clues, and read with increasing understanding • select and use a range of strategies, to make meaning clearer • respond to close reading tasks
Wales	Language, literacy and communication skills	KS 2	• develop word recognition and contextual understanding • develop ability to read with understanding • read in different ways for different purposes • experience a wide range of texts

The Lord of the Rings

Use the following words to complete the passage.

journey	companions	Return	destroying	might	twists	found
voted	regain	screen	again	travelling	language	actors
wizard	director	forces	struggle	creation	landscapes	

The Lord of the Rings by the late J R R Tolkein, a ....(1) professor at Oxford University, has been ....(2) the best book of the 20th century in several worldwide polls. Now, in this century, film-making technology has brought to the ....(3) Tolkein's fantasy trilogy which concludes with The ....(4) of the King. The many fantasy creatures such as Gollum and Treebeard were brought to life using actors and CGI (computer–generated imaging). With these amazing visual effects and using world-famous ....(5) like Cate Blanchett and Elijah Wood, the films have given Tolkein's epic tale to entranced cinema-goers. The ....(6), Peter Jackson, shot all the films back to back in New Zealand. There, the wide variety of ....(7) imaginatively described in Tolkein's books could be ....(8) without the enormous cost of ....(9) around the world to different locations.

The story tells how Gandalf the ....(10), Frodo the Hobbit and their ....(11) set off on a dangerous journey across Middle Earth to save their people by ....(12) the ring of power. They ....(13) through many strange lands, constantly pursued by the ....(14) of the Dark Lord, Sauron and the Creature, Gollum. Sauron and Gollum are both driven to ....(15) possession

of the ring. Sauron needs his ....(16) to return to full power so he ....(17) hold all Middle Earth under his control. Gollum desires once ....(18) to have his 'precious' (the ring). The companions ....(19) against both these foes and against the ring itself, that...................................(20) all it touches, and desires only to return to its creator, Sauron.

Edward Jenner

Smallpox is a disease that once killed millions. It is caused ....(1) spread from person to person through droplets ....(2) when someone coughs or sneezes. Many survivors were blinded or scarred ....(3). The disease was so common ....(4) that almost everyone caught it at some time. ....(5) more soldiers died from smallpox than from fighting, and when European settlers carried the disease ....(6), millions of Native American Indians died.

In the 18th century healthy people were inoculated ....(7) from smallpox sores but it was dangerous as they could develop a serious kind of smallpox.

....(8), Edward Jenner, discovered vaccination (from the Latin 'vacca', meaning 'a cow') as a way of protecting people ....(9). He realised that dairymaids who caught cowpox, ...(10), did not catch smallpox. In 1796 he inoculated James Phipps, a boy aged eight, with pus ....(11) and James caught cowpox. Six weeks later Jenner inoculated him again with smallpox virus and it had no effect ....(12). His experiment was a success!

...................................(13) the World Health Organisation set out to eliminate smallpox altogether. A few years ago the only smallpox viruses left were ....(14) .

- **to North America**
- **for life**
- **with liquid**

- **In 1967**
- **A British doctor**
- **on the boy**

- **from smallpox**
- **in the air**
- **by a virus**
- **in a laboratory**

- **a mild cattle disease**
- **centuries ago**
- **In some wars**

- **from a dairymaid's sore**

Changing Art

Use the following nouns to complete the passage.

paintings	centuries	tombs	lovers	elephants	government
insurance	Romans	film	room	University	world	paint
heroes	complaints	example	people	money	museums	surface

Ancient Egyptian art decorated ....(1) with images of an afterlife. Greek art depicted their gods and mythical ....(2) like Achilles and was admired by the ....(3) who copied it. In the 14th, 15th and 16th ....(4), religious paintings were of the greatest importance.

At one time, ...(5) had to travel to the world's art galleries and ....(6) to see great works of art. Nowadays—though security and ....(7) costs are huge—Rodin's sculptures, ...(8) by Titian and Constable or modernists like Ben Nicholson and Jackson Pollock travel the ....(9) in special exhibitions.

A recent ....(10), Pollock, reminds us of an Australian ....(11) which paid a lot of money for 'Blue Poles'. This is an ....(12) of Pollock's action painting where ....(13) is dripped or thrown onto a horizontal ....(14). Many people protested about the waste of taxpayer's ....(15)—but it is now worth a great deal more!

Some modern sculptures, such as 'Lipstick Ascending on Caterpillar Tracks' at Yale ....(16), have outraged thousands of art ....(17). Britain's websites were flooded with ....(18) when the 2001 Turner Prize winner was a model of an empty ....(19) with a flickering light bulb! We even have popular exhibitions of paintings by ....(20) and chimpanzees! Van Gogh couldn't sell a painting while he was alive but now they are worth millions!

The Milky Way

Our entire Solar System is just a tiny part ....(1) the galaxy called the

Milky Way. Galaxies are large

............................(2) of stars, dust,

gases and planets clustered together.

Our ....(3) Way is

just one of many galaxies existing within ....(4) universe. The Milky Way

contains hundreds of billions of ....(5) and is shaped like a thin disk with a

............................(6) in the centre. From this central bulge are curved ....(7)

of stars, planets and dust forming a spiral shape. ....(8) Milky Way is

known as a spiral galaxy. Our ....(9) System sits on the outer edge of one of

............................(10) spiral arms.

All stars in the Milky Way orbit ....(11) centre just like the planets in our

Solar System ....(12) the Sun. Our Sun completes one orbit of the

............................(13) every 250 million years. The central bulge of the ....(14)

has a vast number of older stars. Both the ....(15) and disk are surrounded by

a sphere of stars ....(16) as a 'halo'. Scientists believe that within the centre

............................(17) that bulge is a large black hole. Black holes ....(18)

invisible objects whose gravitational pull is so great that ....(19) gets sucked

into them, including the light.

Scientists measure ....(20) between stars and galaxies in 'light years'. A light

............................(21) is the distance light travels in one year. Our ....(22) is

one hundred thousand light years across. Light travels ....(23) nearly three

hundred thousand kilometres per second, so these ....(24) are very large.

galaxy	*stars*	*those*	*bulge*	*galaxy*
of	*distances*	*its*	*of*	*at*
groups	*bulge*	*orbit*	*distances*	*Solar*
everything	*known*	*galaxy*	*year*	*The*
the	*arms*	*Milky*	*are*	

Child Stars

Use the following adjectives to complete the passage.

British	endless	troubled	little	normal	famous	humorous
young	sensible	popular	American	cheating	first	paltry
annual	financial	successful	bitter	finest	youngest	

Shirley Temple, ...(1) for her hit song On the Good Ship, Lollipop, made

her ....(2) film at the age of 3. Soon she'd become one of the most

...............................(3) child stars of the last century. Drew Barrymore will always be

remembered as the ....(4) girl Gertie in E.T., while Daniel Radcliffe was the

popular schoolboy, Harry Potter. Macaulay Culkin starred in the ....(5) film

Home Alone, which was a huge hit in the 1990s.

Welsh girl Charlotte Church's CD, Voice of an Angel, made her the ....(6)

artist ever to reach No. 1 in the ....(7) classical charts in 2002. She was a

millionaire at 13 but only had a ....(8) amount of pocket money from her very

...............................(9) parents!

The North ....(10) TV appearances of the Olsen twins, Mary-Kate and Ashley,

at 9 months old, eventually led to a ....(11) TV series. Soon, their enormous

popularity created an ....(12) supply of films, music, software, dolls, books and

clothing. Their ....(13) income is huge!

Child stardom obviously has its ....(14) rewards but no privacy for the

...............................(15) star. Fame for some

of them has led to ....(16)

squabbles with parents or disagreements with

...............................(17) managers over money.

Judy Garland led a ....(18)

life after starring in The Wizard of Oz, one

of the ....(19) children's films.

Perhaps we should be grateful we lead

...............................(20) lives!

Hercules

Hercules is the ....(1) name for the Greek legendary hero Heracles. Myths tell us he was courageous and ....(2). Hera, the wife of Zeus, King of the ancient gods, ...(3) Hercules, as Zeus had fathered him with another woman. She placed two venomous snakes into his ....(4) but the baby strangled them.

As a ....(5) man he was taught archery, wrestling and ....(6) by different experts. Later, in a fit of ....(7) caused by Hera, he killed his wife and children. As a punishment, for twelve years Hercules had to ....(8) the Greek king who made him perform the 'Twelve Labours of Hercules'.

These tasks included the slaying of the multi-headed ....(9) but as he cut off one head two grew in its place. Finally he slew the monster and used its blood to poison his ....(10). For his twelfth task Hercules ....(11) into the world of the dead to capture Cerberus, the three-headed watchdog ....(12) the underworld. Hercules also sailed with Jason in his ....(13) for the Golden Fleece.

When he died, Hercules was ....(14) to Mount Olympus, home of the gods, and became a god. He married a ....(15) of Hera, who had caused him so much trouble throughout his life.

arrows	serve	strong	young
cradle	Roman	search	carried
guarding	madness	descended	hated
daughter	Hydra	music	

Transport in the Future

Use the following words to complete the passage.
You will need to refer to the diagram to fill in some of the spaces.

airports	called	moving	cheaper	roof	metres	air
differ	litres	engines	private	built	huge	personal
deafening	up	Olympics	true	down	weight	

Future modes of transport will ....(1) from those used today. We could

see film fantasies come ....(2) with spaceships linking cities and citizens

on ....(3) 'travelators' winding round city streets. We may use airboards,

.................................(4) hovercraft like those used in Sydney's ....(5). They ride

on a cushion of ....(6) and are driven by a simple petrol engine. Airboards can

only be used on ....(7) land at present as no laws cover them on public roads.

Some cargo planes are ....(8), but Boeing engineers have plans for an even

larger cargo plane ....(9) the Pelican. Its wingspan is 150

.................................(10), the wings slope ....(11), it has four ....(12)

and is twice the size of the Russian AN 225. The Pelican's ....(13) would

prevent it taking off from Starrports, which are possible future ....(14), named

after their designer, Jim Starry. Planes take off from a Starrport's ....(15), then

along a shortened runway with a 1% slope. The slope means a Jumbo jet would save over

1300 ....(16) of fuel. When landing ....(17) the slope, gravity halts

the plane with huge fuel savings and no need for the ....(18) reverse thrust of

the engines.

Sea travel, once ....(19)

than air travel, will see even bigger cruise

ships carrying thousands of passengers.

In 2002, forty-two new ships were being

.................................(20), some weighing over

100 000 tonnes like the QMII, the world's

largest passenger ship, whose maiden

voyage was in 2004!

The Solar System

Our Solar System exists within a vast universe. It ....(1) part of the galaxy called the Milky Way. The ....(2) System is shaped like a disk. It consists of ....(3) star called the Sun and all the objects that ....(4) around it. These objects include eight planets, a dwarf planet and their ....(5), meteoroids, asteroids, comets and dust.

The Sun is the ....(6) of our Solar System. It is about six hundred ....(7) bigger than all the objects in the Solar System ....(8) together. Each planet varies in size and distance from ....(9) Sun, with the exception of Pluto, whose path crosses ....(10) the orbital path of Neptune. The order of the ....(11) from the closest to the furthest away from the ....(12) is Mercury, Venus, Earth, Mars, Jupiter, Saturn, Uranus, Neptune ....(13) Pluto (the dwarf planet).

Thousands of minor planets, called asteroids, also orbit ....(14) Sun. These small objects are made from metal or ....(15). Many of them are found circling the Sun in ....(16) broad 'asteroid belt' between the orbits of Mars and ....(17). Asteroids can also be known as planetoids. Meteoroids are ....(18) pieces of rock, metal or gas after the collision ....(19) asteroids or the breaking up of a comet. Comets ....(20) small bodies made of frozen gases with a long ....(21) of dust and gases that escape from the head ....(22) nucleus.

or	and	the	are	times	
a	rock	over	tail	put	Sun
Solar	left-over	centre	travel	the	Jupiter
moons	a	of	is	planets	

Mobile Phones

Use your own words to complete the passage.
Use a word only once and use a single word in each space.

Early mobile phones were quite big but the latest can be hidden in the ....(1)

of your hand. One new phone has a built-in ....(2) camera that takes still

or ....(3) images which can be sent without ....(4) any

other software. Like a tiny computer, it can surf the ....(5) and read your

emails. The handset can download a language translator to help an overseas traveller

to ....(6) a foreign menu. It can even be used to ....(7) the

restaurant bill in the local currency!

Language, from ancient Egyptian hieroglyphs to our ....(8) alphabet,

is important for communication. Short Message Service (SMS) text is a shortened

...............................(9) of English used to send text messages by ....(10)

phones. It uses letters and ....(11) so that 'URL8' (only four characters)

replaces 'you are ....(12)'. Mobile phones can only use a certain number of

...............................(13) before becoming too expensive so a new truncated

...............................(14) was needed. Many millions of SMS ....(15) are now sent

every month by teenagers alone using this modern text form.

Hundreds of medical research programmes are still investigating possible ....(16) risks associated with mobile phones. One head of the World Health Organisation has ....(17) parents about overuse by their ....(18). Despite these fears, most ....(19) value the phones as a contact in emergencies. Many ....(20), however, see them as a nuisance in class—and they are banned from examination rooms.

Communications History

Humans have always used ....(1) ways of communicating. Primitive tribes drew pictures on cave walls and this ....(2) kind of written communication has been found in Spain, France and Australia. Native North Americans used picture writing but, living on ....(3) land, also used smoke signals visible over ....(4) distances. African tribes in ....(5) jungles, where they couldn't see far, used drums. Long ago, ...(6) notches on message sticks or knots on string provided information carried by runners.

Army leaders have used carrier pigeons and navies developed a system of signalling with ....(7) flags called semaphore. Armies also used heliographs, which were mirrors that reflected the sun, to send long or ....(8) flashes of light. Helios was the sun-god in myths of the ancient Greeks who used ....(9) metal to reflect the sun's rays.

Now we have satellites, television, fax machines, ...(10) computer networks and the telephone invented by Bell in 1876. The invention of printing in the 15th century led to ....(11) books and newspapers.

Scientists using optical fibres the thickness of a ....(12) hair now send faster messages. Beams of light called lasers change the ....(13) signals of phone calls or TV pictures into light impulses. Lasers then send the light along ....(14) fibres over great distances without losing strength. At the receiving end, machines change the laser light back to the ....(15) message.

polished	worldwide	human	coloured
carved	electrical	long	modern
flat	short	earliest	glass
original	different	dense	

The Sun

The Sun is by far the largest object

in ....(1) Solar

System. It is an enormous ball of

hot, ...(2) gas which

is the centre of our Solar System.

....................(3) the planets

travel around it at different speeds. It ....(4) to be big and bright; however,

it is not ....(5) largest star in the galaxy. The Sun is 150 ....(6)

kilometres away from Earth. Light from the Sun takes ....(7) minutes to reach

us, whereas light from the next ....(8) star, Sirius, takes eight years! Scientists

call our Sun ....(9) 'yellow dwarf'. Some stars are over 1000 times larger

....................(10) our Sun and are called 'supergiants'.

The Sun is ....(11) up of gases, mostly hydrogen and some helium.

At ....(12) centre, or core, the Sun's temperatures are around fifteen

....................(13) degrees Celsius. Scientists think that the Sun has shone

....................(14) the sky for nearly five billion years and believe ....(15)

has enough hydrogen fuel to 'burn' for another five ....(16) six billion years.

This giant star gives our Earth ....(17) light and heat needed for survival on our

planet. ....(18) the Sun there would be no life on Earth. ....(19)

use the Sun's light when making their food. When ....(20) plant does this,

it gives off oxygen. Animals eat ....(21) plants and breathe the oxygen. The

animals then breathe ....(22) carbon dioxide which the plants combine

with the Sun's ....(23) and water to make more food, continuing the cycle

....................(24) life on our planet.

million	*eight*	*the*	*million*	*to*	*out*
our	*a*	*Plants*	*in*	*All*	*light*
the	*glowing*	*it*	*than*	*a*	*nearest*
appears	*made*	*the*	*Without*	*the*	*of*

Bullying

Use the following words to complete the poem.
The poem uses rhyming couplets which means that
each pair of successive lines end in rhyming words.

ease	games	school	peers	tall
see	lose	beware	TV	schools	all
rules	tears	aware	names	tease
choose	outside	cruel	denied

Of bullying today we are more .... (1),

Schools have strategies, so bullies .... (2)!

Taunting, abuse and calling .... (3)

The bully's excuse—just playing .... (4)!

We picture the bully as strong and .... (5)

But that may not be the culprit at .... (6),

Frail-looking bullies can slyly .... (7)

Their nasty tales make pupils ill at .... (8),

They can isolate socially someone they .... (9)

So these lonely targets have friends they can .... (10)

The bully—poor role models, outside of .... (11)?

Conditioned by elders both unfair and .... (12)?

Perhaps they don't fit in, or there's pressure from .... (13)

Is that an excuse to reduce classmates to .... (14)?

Do they view these examples in films, on .... (15)?

Is it aggressive behaviours we want them to .... (16)?

Parents and teachers should discuss forming .... (17),

Work hard to discourage this scourge in our .... (18),

Make school policies known in school and .... (19)

So each pupil's rights cannot be .... (20).

Television

Many scientists contributed to the development of television .... (1) of the 20th century. One we remember is John Logie Baird, ...(2) , who gave the first public demonstration of television in England in 1926 and colour pictures ....(3). Australian TV award statuettes are named 'Logies' ....(4).

To obtain television pictures, the light ....(5) is taken in by a television camera which then changes the light ....(6). A microphone picks up the sounds ....(7) and changes those to electronic signals too. The camera's 'video' signals go ....(8) and the microphone's 'audio' signals go to a loudspeaker. These signals are picked up ....(9) and our TV sets change the audio and video signals ....(10) recorded by the camera and microphone.

Many TV signals are transmitted ....(11) along electromagnetic waves which travel at 300 000 km per second, the speed of light. Pictures sent this way can only travel a distance of 250 kilometres. To send pictures ....(12) other methods are used such as microwaves or satellites like Telstar or Earlybird, launched in the 1960's.

Television links people around the world ....(13) and entertainment and is also a valuable educational tool. However, there is a lot of criticism ....(14) about the sex and violence that can be watched ....(15) whose viewing habits are not supervised by parents.

- **through the air**
- **two years later**
- **by young people**
- **from a scene**
- **in the early years**
- **into electronic signals**
- **back to the original pictures**
- **within communities**
- **at the same time**
- **to news items**
- **to a picture tube**
- **over greater distances**
- **a Scottish engineer**
- **by our aerials**
- **in his honour**

Body Image

Use your own words to complete the passage.
Select one word for each space and do not use a word more than once.

Recent studies ....(1) that attractive children are popular with classmates and

..............................(2) at school, and attractive job applicants have a ....(3) chance

of success. This 'bias for beauty' is even ....(4) in our literature—wicked

stepmothers or cruel sisters are ....(5) but good fairies are beautiful.

TV commercials, magazines and films show images of handsome stars or

..............................(6) models. The slimness of many models is ....(7) to achieve

for the average adult or teenager, so low self-esteem may ....(8) to anorexia

or bulimia, both ....(9) to a person's health. Men are less self-critical, with

..............................(10) of hair and lack of height ....(11) of their main worries.

Recent studies in America and Sweden found many primary ....(12) girls had

dieted in order to ....(13) weight and almost half of Japanese primary pupils

..............................(14) they were too fat. Boys are less critical of their ....(15)

except during adolescence. Any teasing of their appearance when young may permanently

affect children's ....(16) image but school educational programmes can help

..............................(17) to accept who they are.

'Beauty is in the eye of the beholder' said Margaret Hungerford and perceptions vary from culture to ....(18). 'Giraffe' women with metal bands wrapped ....(19) elongated necks or other native women with a large plate stretching their lower lip are ....(20) attractive within their own culture.

Mercury

Mercury is the closest planet to the Sun and ....(1) less than half the size of the Earth. Due ....(2) Mercury's size and closeness to the Sun's bright glare, ...(3) is often hard to see from the Earth without ....(4) telescope.

Mercury travels around the Sun in an elliptical ....(5) and moves faster than any other planet. The ancient ....(6) named the planet after the 'swift messenger' of their ....(7), probably because it travelled so quickly across the sky. ....(8) takes only 88 days to travel around the Sun ....(9). The Earth takes just over 365 days to do ....(10) same thing. Mercury rotates slowly on its axis, so ....(11) day on Mercury is almost as long as sixty ....(12) days.

The surface of Mercury is very much like ....(13) of our Moon. It has steep cliffs, flat plains ....(14) many deep craters. Many scientists believe these craters were ....(15) by meteorites and comets hitting its surface. Mercury is ....(16) dry, hot and has no real air. The temperature ....(17) the planet's surface may reach as high as 420°C: ....(18) enough to melt lead. As there is a lack ....(19) atmosphere, Mercury's sky is black and stars would probably ....(20) visible from its surface by day. On the dark ....(21), facing away from the Sun, or at night, temperatures ....(22) drop to -173°C: colder than the Earth's South Pole. ....(23) of the plant or animal life on Earth could ....(24) on Mercury due to the intense temperatures and the ....(25) of oxygen.

is	*Romans*	*a*	*very*	*side*
to	*gods*	*Earth*	*on*	*can*
it	*It*	*that*	*hot*	*None*
a	*once*	*and*	*of*	*survive*
orbit	*the*	*formed*	*be*	*lack*

Limited Overs Cricket

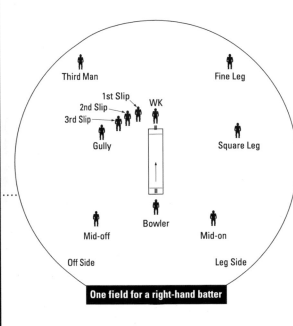

Third Man
Fine Leg
1st Slip
2nd Slip
3rd Slip
WK
Gully
Square Leg
Bowler
Mid-off
Mid-on
Off Side
Leg Side

One field for a right-hand batter

Use the following words to complete the passage. You will need to refer to the diagram to fill in some of the spaces.

Apart   colourful   popular   gully   critics   players   different   three   part   matches   played   result   involved   slips   millions   supporters   main   International   third   form

The first one-day game was ....(1) in England in 1963 and then introduced to international ....(2). It has gained enormous popularity and has been the ....(3) source of revenue for the countries ....(4). In cricket-mad India it has become far more ....(5) than Test cricket and new competitors like Bangladesh, Zimbabwe and Kenya are now ....(6) of the world programme. Outstanding ....(7) such as Adam Gilchrist, Sachin Tendulkar and Brian Lara have ....(8) of fans around the globe. Women also play this ....(9) of the game and Australia's Belinda Clark has a record score of 229 not out for a one-day ....(10).

Test cricketers wear white but because of the ....(11) clothing worn in one-day matches, ...(12) have often referred to it as 'cricket in pyjamas'! However, ...(13) love the game as they know they'll see a ....(14) the day they attend.

Some rules are ....(15) from Test cricket but positions in the field are the same. In the field shown there are three ....(16) and if the ball is snicked through them, the ....(17) man should prevent a boundary. ....(18) from the wicket-keeper, ...(19) is the only position near the slips and there are only ....(20) fielders on the leg side.

Dinosaurs

The word dinosaur comes from two Greek words meaning '......................................(1) lizard'. They lived over 200 million years ago. Scientists learn about them by ....(2) fossils, which are animal remains that have hardened into rock after millions of years under the ....(3). People have found fossil dinosaur eggs and trace fossils which are often animal ....(4) left in rock layers. When fossil bones are found they are covered with plaster or foam for ....(5). We can also learn about dinosaurs by studying other ....(6) land animals like elephants.

In 1822 an English doctor's ....(7) found a large fossil tooth. She showed it to her husband, who ....(8) fossils, and he realised it was a new kind of creature. Since then, remains have been discovered around the ....(9). When found, fossil skeletons are carefully ....(10) and then assembled on metal frames. Broken parts are repaired or replaced with pieces made from ....(11), plaster or fibreglass.

Scientists do not know why dinosaurs ....(12). One theory is that a giant asteroid hit the earth and raised huge ....(13) of dust. These blocked out sunlight for several years and killed ....(14). With no food for themselves or the animals they ....(15), dinosaurs died too.

cleaned	disappeared	collected	clouds	studying
ground	ate	footprints	world	protection
terrible	wife	huge	plants	plastic

Extreme Sports

Use the following adjectives to complete the passage.

several	high-rise	individual	broken	serious	local	obvious
physical	Extreme	various	important	dangerous		long
particular	in-line	greatest	firm	artificial	every	increasing

..............................(1) sports include excitement, skills and danger with ....(2) activities below ground, in the air and on the water. Most are ....(3) sports rather than team events, with participants trying to avoid the ....(4) dangers but enjoying the thrills. Sydney's 2000 Olympics was for the ....(5) athletes, but in December 2002 Sydney also hosted the Planet X Games for Extreme Sports stars from ....(6) parts of the world.

Base jumping—that is, parachuting from ....(7) buildings, bridges etc.— is the most ....(8) of these sports which include hang-gliding, BMX, ...(9) skating, skateboarding and surfing. One skateboarder in 1998 was timed at 100 km/h and ....(10) year doctors treat thousands of youngsters for ....(11) bones or fractures, with spinal injuries from surfing accidents adding to the ....(12) injury list. Quality protective equipment is very ....(13), especially helmets to protect the head and ....(14) shin or elbow pads to prevent ....(15) abrasions.

Authorities in ....(16) countries have built bike tracks, skateboard facilities or ....(17) surfing reefs to cater for the ....(18) popularity of extreme sports. If you'd like to read more about a ....(19) extreme sport, you only need to look in your ....(20) newsagency. There you will find an array of magazines catering for extreme sport enthusiasts.

Neptune

Neptune, known as Poseidon to the Ancient Greeks, was the most important god of the sea in Roman ....(1). The Romans believed he had ....(2) over the seas and sailors who sailed them. They thought he could cause violent ....(3), or prevent them to protect sailors. At Neptune festivals each July, Roman citizens feasted and drank ....(4).

The Romans were a seafaring ....(5) who imported many goods by ship so a sea god was important in their daily ....(6). Sea travel was dangerous in those ....(7) because of their small ships, so sailors often prayed to Neptune for protection.

Neptune was the son of ....(8) and Ops. He married a sea nymph, a female spirit, and had a child called Triton who was half man and half ....(9).

Artists often show Neptune carrying a three-pronged ....(10), a hunting weapon popular with Mediterranean ....(11). In some paintings, apart from the trident, he is shown carrying a ....(12), to remind worshippers he is also the god of horses. Many ....(13) have a statue of Neptune, including the Trevi fountain which is a popular tourist attraction in ....(14).

The planet Neptune was named after this Roman god and its largest ....(15) after Neptune's son.

fishermen	moon	spear	power	lives
wine	people	Rome	storms	fish
Saturn	myths	times	fountains	whip

Recycling

Use the following words to complete the passage.

supplies   roads   technology   expensive
lifted   reduces   regulations   cartons   bacteria
drunk   food   household   small   required
paper   recycled   fires   Europe   washes   find

By recycling ....(1) we save

our trees, but we can also recycle glass

bottles, milk ....(2) and plastic.

Recycling conserves many non-renewable

resources and ....(3)

greenhouse gas emissions because local

councils send less ....(4) waste to landfill sites. It also means less energy is

..............................(5) when making new materials from old.

Health ....(6) once prevented recycled plastic from being used for

..............................(7) containers but new technology has seen this ban ....(8)

in some countries.

Sewage and stormwater collected from ....(9) and the roofs of buildings,

is also ....(10). Water treatment plants treat millions of litres a day,

removing ....(11) and unwanted particles. This recycled water can't be

..............................(12) or used for cooking but is able to be used for car ....(13),

flushing toilets, watering parks and fighting ....(14). This means there is a

reduced demand on drinking water ....(15).

New ....(16) is constantly improving recycling

techniques in ....(17), America and Japan, but

countries with ....(18) populations like Australia

or Belgium may ....(19) these new developments

are too ....(20) to use in the immediate future.

The Moon

The Moon is the Earth's closest neighbour in space. ....[1] the Moon is the brightest object in the night ....[2] it does not give off its own light. The '.............................'[3] is only a reflection of light from the Sun. ....[4] the Earth was the size of a golf ball ....[5] Moon would be the size of a marble. As ....[6] Moon is a lot smaller than the Earth, its ....[7] is also a lot less. A person who weighs ....[8] on Earth will weigh only 10 kg on the Moon.

.................................[9] though the Moon and Earth are very close to ....[10] other in space, they are very different from each ....[11]. The Earth is a blue, watery, cloud-covered planet, filled ....[12] living things. The Moon is a barren place with ....[13] water, air, clouds or living things. The Moon's surface ....[14] covered by thousands of bowl-shaped craters, thought to be ....[15] by meteorites or asteroids crashing into the Moon. The ....[16] is also covered with mountains, hills, valleys and flat ....[17]. The temperature can vary between -240°C and 130°C.

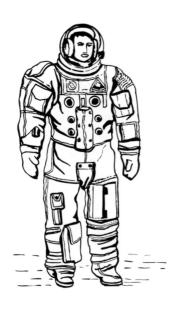

More ....[18] known about our Moon than any other object in ....[19], as it is the only object in space to ....[20] visited by humans. In 1969, Neil Armstrong became the ....[21] person to set foot on the Moon. He was ....[22] of three astronauts aboard the spacecraft *Apollo 11* that ....[23] on the Moon on 20 July 1969. Other successful ....[24] followed, providing a means of studying the Moon in ....[25] accurate detail.

other	*the*	*be*	*moonlight*	*more*
sky	*plains*	*the*	*first*	*with*
gravity	*is*	*Although*	*one*	*expeditions*
If	*space*	*60 kg*	*surface*	*is*
landed	*Even*	*each*	*no*	*formed*

Robots

Use the following verbs to complete the passage.

searched   assemble   led   Equipped
destroyed   solve   distinguish   produced
weld   approach   find   interacts   are
walked   programmed   recognises
reacts   mow   understand   driven

Recent developments in electronics and computer technology have ....[1] to important advances in robotics. Humanoids ....[2] human-like machines with mechanical arms and legs. In 2001, secret research by Japan's Honda company ....[3] one the size of a 10-year-old child. Guided by remote control, it ....[4] and could grasp objects.

Today, one-armed industrial robots are used to ....[5] and spraypaint car body parts, and some can even ....[6] electronic circuits and tiny parts in watches. The different movements required are ....[7] into the robot's memory. Robots are also used to ....[8] and defuse terrorist bombs. ....[9] with cameras and electronic touch sensors, three small robots similar to remote-control model cars ....[10] for victims among the rubble of New York's Twin Towers after the terrorist attack ....[11] them.

'Kismet', ...[12] by 15 computers, is the world's first robot which ....[13] with people because it ....[14] their moods through the varying pitch of their speech. Though it can't ....[15] what is said, Kismet recognises a sad or angry voice and ....[16] to it with appropriate gestures.

Though future robots will ....[17] our lawns and vacuum our homes, engineers ....[18] that designing a robot even to ....[19] an egg from a book or bottle is still a major problem to ....[20].

The Tiger

In 1900 there were about 40 000 ....(1)
tigers in India. Now there are less than 7000 in
the ....(2) world. At a
wildlife protection meeting of more
than one hundred nations in Florida
in 1994, ...(3)
Asian countries, including China and
Japan, proposed greater protection
for these ....(4)
animals. Unfortunately, it is in these
....(5) countries that
'Jinbou' is widespread. This is the ancient
belief that taking medicines prepared from animal parts will improve ....(6)
health.

Almost all parts of the tiger are used: the eyes for malaria or fever in ....(7)
children; its whiskers for toothache; tiger bone preparations for ....(8)
joints; its teeth for asthma; its fat for vomiting and ....(9) dog bites and its
tail for skin diseases. Its beautiful ....(10) coat was once popular for rugs
but import bans on such items mean ....(11) poachers often leave the skins
and take the more ....(12) parts for use in oriental medicines. This trade has
been extremely ....(13) in ....(14) years.

Let us hope you still have the opportunity to see tigers roaming wild in
....(15) jungles when you are an adult.

poor	tropical	Asian	striped	recent
painful	aching	entire	cruel	valuable
magnificent	profitable	young	ten	wild

Comets

Comets are icy balls that travel through our Solar ....(1), orbiting the Sun. The

centre of a comet is ....(2) hard, icy core called a nucleus. A cloudy atmosphere

..........................(3) the nucleus and is called a coma. Together, the ....(4) and

coma form the head of a comet. The ....(5) of the comet looks a little like a dirty

..........................(6) of snow. This ball may be less than 16 ....(7) in diameter and

is made from frozen gases, ice ....(8) pieces of rock dust. The gases include

ammonia, carbon ....(9), carbon monoxide and methane.

Each time a comet passes ....(10) to the Sun it loses some of its ice

..........................(11) dust. The solar winds blow a stream of gas ....(12) dust

away from the comet and away from the ....(13). This forms the comet's

tail. This is a spectacular ....(14) of gas and dust that can trail for millions

..........................(15) kilometres into space.

Some comets eventually lose all their ....(16) and dust. They then become

clouds of dust or ....(17) into asteroids. Some pieces of comets can reach the

..........................(18). As they pass through our atmosphere they burn up ....(19)

are called 'meteors' or 'shooting stars'.

Comets are usually ....(20) only with a telescope but sometimes, when one is

..........................(21) to the Sun, we can see it without a ....(22) for several days

or even weeks. There are many ....(23) in our system but the best known is

Halley's ....(24). It was named after Edmund Halley

when he successfully ....(25) its return in 1758 to

our skies. He recognised ....(26) this comet could be

seen on average every 77 ....(27) as it orbits the Sun.

The comet is now ....(28) the orbit of Uranus and is

expected to return ....(29) the year 2062.

comets	*and*	*predicted*	*turn*
surrounds	*dioxide*	*close*	*Earth*
that	*nucleus*	*and*	*kilometres*
a	*centre*	*ice*	*and*
Comet	*ball*	*System*	*seen*

close	*in*	*Sun*
years	*telescope*	*streak*
beyond	*and*	*of*

High-speed Trains

Since the days of George Stephenson's 1829 Rocket, a steam locomotive, engineers have tried to ....(1) faster trains. The world's fastest trains using ....(2) wheels, modified tracks and overhead ....(3) have been France's TGV (trains a la grande vitesse) and Japan's 'bullet trains'.

Engineers around the world have been developing high-speed ....(4) levitation trains ('maglevs') and an early Japanese test model, ML-500, has ....(5) over 500 km/h. One type of maglev has an electrodynamic system and glides ....(6) the track using magnetic repulsion—seen when the 'like' poles of two ....(7) repel each other in classroom experiments. Magnets on the underside of the maglev create ....(8) in wire coils or metal plates set in the track (the 'guideway'). The ....(9) is lifted about 10 cm above the guideway by the opposing magnetic forces. The moving currents push the train forward like ocean ....(10) pushing a surfer along. Another type of maglev uses electromagnetic forces where magnetic ....(11) rather than repulsion is used.

In 2003, a new high-speed maglev linked Shanghai ....(12) to the city, but tickets are very ....(13). In the not too distant future, maglev trains travelling at 500 km/h are ....(14) to compete with planes on some routes and Germany and ....(15) already use low-speed maglevs. Because there is no ....(16) with the guideway, the rides are very smooth and ....(17). As there is no surface-to-surface friction, the guideways need little ....(18) and because maglevs use electric ....(19), there is a minimal pollution of the ....(20).

The Motor Car

Early powered carriages were

.....................................(1) by steam. In 1885 German

engineers, Daimler and Benz, ...(2)

the first successful petrol-driven cars. These engines

.....................................(3) power when a mixture of fuel and air ....(4) inside

the engine. Early electric cars were quiet and pollution free but their batteries had to be

.....................................(5) after about 50 km.

Road safety regulations were ....(6) in 1865 and someone had to walk in

front of any self-propelled carriage with a red flag or a red lantern to ....(7)

pedestrians.

The first cars were ....(8) by hand by skilled craftsmen but Henry

Ford wanted cheaper cars and developed an assembly line in 1914. Workers

.....................................(9) on either side of a moving belt and ....(10) the

different parts to the T-model Ford chassis as it passed by. Today, in many countries, robots

have ....(11) these workers on assembly lines.

The electric starter replaced starting handles, and pneumatic tyres with their cushion

of air ....(12) rides more comfortable. Safety glass that didn't

.....................................(13) into dangerous splinters was introduced in the 1920's.

More streamlined solar-powered or electric cars of the future will reduce the danger from

lead or benzene in the air we ....(14). Cars have changed our lifestyle but

.....................................(15) thousands of people on the world's roads each year.

shatter	**developed**	**stood**	**added**
gain	**explodes**	**kill**	**built**
replaced	**driven**	**recharged**	**passed**
breathe	**made**	**warn**	

Exploring the Ocean Depths

Use the following adjectives to complete the passage.

major	recent	normal	marine	upper	similar	lifeless	American
terrible	electric	several	useful	industrial	enormous		popular
possible		unknown		amazing		sophisticated	toxic

Many scientists regard the ocean bed as the last ....[1] frontier on Earth

with ....[2] oil and mineral deposits. Research has also shown that

..................................[3] creatures attached to the sea floor produce defence chemicals which

could be ....[4] in the treatment of cancer.

The lungs of deep-sea divers can't withstand the ....[5] pressure of the

water above, but the 'newtsuit' enables them to work at depths of 300 m. They breathe air at

..................................[6] pressure supplied from a backpack system so they don't have to spend

..................................[7] days in a decompression chamber to avoid

a ....[8] sickness called 'the bends'.

Oceanographers also use bathyscaphes, submersibles

propelled by an ....[9] motor and designed to

withstand great pressures. The modern Spider, a one-man

underwater craft, is ....[10] to Bushnell's 1776

Turtle used against British vessels in the ....[11] War of Independence.

Ocean exploration has led to the development of ....[12] camera, video

and lighting systems so that ....[13] pictures of the Titanic 4 km below the

Atlantic waves have appeared in ....[14] magazines and on television. Using

'deep rovers' in ....[15] dives, some Australian scientists identified over 700

previously ....[16] fish species.

Oceans have been viewed by some ....[17] nations as mere dumping grounds.

After World War II, ...[18] wastes were dumped into the Baltic Sea. Marine

scientists recently found that only the ....[19] levels of that sea contain

oxygen. Deeper levels are so full of foul-smelling hydrogen sulphide the waters are virtually

..................................[20]. Our oceans must be protected in the 21st century.

Meteors

Meteors are bright streaks of light that can be ....(1) at times in our skies. They are often called '........................(2) stars' or 'falling stars'. A meteor can be seen ....(3) a piece of metal or rock, called a meteoroid, ...(4) the atmosphere of Earth at a very high speed. ....(5) friction heats the meteoroid so that it is glowing ....(6) and leaves a trail of hot glowing gases. This ....(7) for only a few seconds. Only a few meteoroids ....(8) reach the surface of the Earth. If they do ....(9) are called meteorites. Millions of meteors enter the atmosphere ....(10) the Earth every day but very few of them ....(11) become meteorites.

Meteoroids travel in a variety of orbits ....(12) speeds around the Sun and enter the Earth's atmosphere ....(13) speeds from 11 km/h to 72 km/h.

There are two different ....(14) of meteorites—stony and iron. Stony meteorites consist of ....(15) minerals and iron particles combined. Iron meteorites consist mainly ....(16) iron with traces of nickel and other elements. Some ....(17) be the size of a marble while others may ....(18) up to 60 tonnes. A meteorite must be of ....(19) size to reach the Earth. If it is too ....(20) it will burn up before it reaches the Earth's ....(21). If it's too big it may explode before reaching ....(22) ground.

Scientists collect and study meteorites as they are ....(23) to be made of material unchanged since the time ....(24) the planets and moons were formed. Thousands of small ....(25) have been found in Antarctica because they have been ....(26) in the ice.

enters	**and**	**at**	**types**	**rock**	**of**	**actually**
may	**substantial**	**Air**	**thought**	**hot**		**lasts**
surface	**that**	**meteorites**	**seen**	**shooting**	**when**	**the**
preserved	**they**	**of**	**ever**	**small**		**weigh**

Protecting Our Borders

Use the following adverbs to complete the passage.

gradually   heavily   always   horrifyingly   almost   given

adequately   strictly   unsuccessfully   easily   often   badly   specially

obviously   now   foolishly   secretly   cruelly   recently   Fortunately

Customs officers have ....(1) tried to detect those people who

..............................(2) try to break a country's border laws, which are ....(3)

enforced. These offenders are ....(4) caught smuggling in the seeds of

banned plants or ....(5) concealing exotic creatures to sell overseas. A rare

parrot or lizard can ....(6) be sold. Only ....(7), a man flying

from Melbourne to Vienna tried ....(8) to smuggle 60 geckos in a trade which

..............................(9) seeks profit and shows no interest in ....(10)

protecting unique wildlife. Offenders can be fined ....(11) and

..............................(12) jail sentences. We all know drugs ....(13) affect

so many lives and some Asian countries have very severe penalties for those who

..............................(14) try to smuggle drugs through their Customs.

Since the 2001 ....(15) brutal terrorist attack on New York and the Bali

bombs in 2002, Customs departments worldwide have ....(16) increased the

number of sniffer dogs able to detect explosives. Many airports and seaports have teams of

..............................(17) trained dogs which

can ....(18) detect over 19 000

explosives combinations!

..............................(19), new X-ray machines

with a much improved capacity will reduce

the chances of smuggling explosives,

weapons or drugs into the country to

..............................(20) nil.

The First Fleet

This English fleet of eleven ships carried the

.....................................(1) British convicts to Australia, setting sail from Portsmouth in May,

1787 under Captain Arthur Phillip in his flagship 'Sirius'. Over 700 ....(2)

convicts were carried below decks in ....(3) ships called transports. The

fleet also carried children, soldiers and animals.

Phillip took fruit and vegetables to prevent scurvy, a ....(4) disease

which killed thousands of sailors. Green vegetables were also grown on board on

.....................................(5) strips of cloth. The Canary Islands, Rio de Janeiro and Cape Town

were three ....(6) ports of call on the difficult voyage to Botany Bay. There

they picked up ....(7) water, food and animals and repaired damage caused

in ....(8) storms.

Phillip and his advance party didn't think Botany Bay would make a ....(9)

settlement. Fresh water was ....(10) and the soil was too poor to grow crops

to support a ....(11) colony. The bay was open to the sea, so strong winds

could be ....(12) for ships.

Phillip sailed north up the coast and found the ....(13) Port Jackson

harbour where Sydney stands today. The tank stream in Sydney Cove provided water, and

.....................................(14) water up to the shore made it easy to unload ships. Phillip then

claimed the ....(15) coast for Britain on 26th January, 1788.

dangerous	welcome	first	leaky	suitable
east	new	terrible	magnificent	fresh
miserable	deep	violent	damp	scarce

Global Warming

Use the following words to complete the passage.
You will need to use the graph to fill in some of the spaces.

graph	populations	responsible	emissions	India	paying
changes	temperature	Canada	trees	annually	rise	aim
countries	support	thirty-six	America	Japan	country	earnt

The Kyoto Pact, developed in Kyoto, Japan, in 1997, aimed to cut ....[1] of

the greenhouse gas carbon dioxide, which some scientists blame for raising the Earth's

................................[2]. Research alleges 'global warming' has led to a thinner Arctic icecap.

Scientists who ....[3] the greenhouse gas theory predict sea levels could

................................[4] by almost a metre this century and threaten ....[5] in

low-lying areas. Other scientists see current higher temperature levels as a part of natural

cyclical ....[6] which are not influenced by humans and which have always

affected us.

The updated pact has now been signed by many ....[7], including high-

emission Asian nations such as Japan, China and ....[8]. The original pact

had to be approved by any group of nations ....[9] for at least 55% of the 1990

emissions. The ....[10] shows America's contribution was

................................[11]%, four times the emissions from ....[12] and twelve times

the percentage for ....[13].

If industrial nations can't reduce their emissions, they can at least plant ....[14],

as just one hectare of forest can absorb over 100 tonnes of carbon ....[15].

These 'carbon credits' can be ....[16] by planting trees in their own country or

................................[17] another government to plant in their available areas.

In 2002, ...[18], said to be the worst

polluter, had not signed the pact, as President Bush

said it was against the 'economic best interests' of

his ....[19]. However, perhaps the best

outcome for the entire planet should be the world's

................................[20] in this century!

Percentages of CO₂ emissions from
industrial countries in 1990

Canada
Australia and New Zealand
Eastern Europe
Japan
Russia
European Union
US

0 5 10 15 20 25 30 35
percentages

Spring

Spring is a ....(1) that many like best,

When all naked trees begin to show ....(2),

Birds ....(3) twigs to build a nest,

Migrating swallows – ....(4) have they been?

Nights grow ....(5), warmer days,

Cricket bats swung by ....(6) in white,

No discomfort from a ....(7) sun's rays,

Daffodils in garden beds, a ....(8) sight!

The morning quiet ....(9) by machines on lawns,

Houses spring cleaned, the ....(10) done,

Bright red sunsets and glowing ....(11),

Everyone's ....(12) for winter's now gone.

Freshly painted boats glide on ....(13) seas,

The bleating of ....(14) as they frolic in the lea,

Brightly coloured ....(15) compete with the bees,

Spring is alive for the world to see!

happy	*hot*	*smooth*	*dawns*	*players*
where	*shorter*	*lambs*	*washing*	*gather*
time	*broken*	*colourful*	*green*	*butterflies*

Water is Precious

Use the following verbs to complete the passage.

import	soak	performed	found	attempted	producing	help
turn	provide	opened	fix	want	depend	put
water	possessed	predicts	lies	collect	survive	

Water is ....[1] in huge quantities on the Earth's surface and underground, but most ....[2] in salty oceans or frozen glaciers and icecaps. Only about 1% is useable fresh water. UNESCO ....[3] that by 2020 there will be a worldwide shortage. In past years, people ....[4] rain dances and scientists around the world 'seeded' dark clouds with chemicals as they ....[5] to bring rain.

Now, desalination plants worldwide ....[6] seawater into quality drinking water. Saudi Arabia's plants ....[7] the country with a liquid more precious than its oil, for people can ....[8] weeks without food but only a few days without water.

Some areas in Australia can't ....[9] gardens with sprinklers during most daylight hours. Parts of California ....[10] on winter rains and during droughts they have to ....[11] expensive water from the Colorado River. Some American coastal cities are considering desalination plants and Tampa, Florida, ...[12] America's first major plant in 2003, ...[13] over 100 million litres of water a day. These cities ....[14] sufficient water supplies but huge population increases ....[15] pressure on resources, and nowadays more people ....[16] automatic washing machines, second bathrooms, spas and so on.

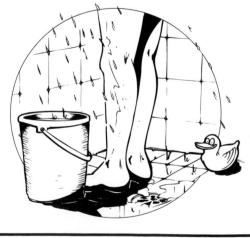

Families can ....[17] at home: replace lawns, which can ....[18] up 50% of domestic water, with drought-resistant plants; use half flushes in toilets; ....[19] leaky taps; take short showers and use a bucket to ....[20] excess shower water! Every drop helps!

Florence Nightingale

Florence Nightingale was born in 1820 of wealthy British parents living in Florence, Italy, but spent her ....(1) in England. Her parents were horrified when she became a nurse, as nursing in those ....(2) was not a respected profession. Later, she was asked to take a ....(3) of nurses to the Crimea in 1854 where ....(4) and France were fighting Russia.

In Scutari they found over 5000 sick and wounded men and a filthy ....(5) infested with rats. She and her nurses improved ....(6) so much that very few ....(7) died from then on. Florence regularly checked the wounded at night and became known as 'the lady with the ....(8)'. She improved hospital treatment for ordinary soldiers who were not ....(9).

After the Crimean War she refused all ....(10) and honours. The public donated large sums of ....(11) because of her work in the war and she used it to begin the Nightingale Training ....(12) for nurses in London.

An ....(13) she had caught during the war made her an invalid and she gradually became blind. In 1907 she became the first ....(14) to be awarded the Order of Merit by a British government. She died in London in 1910 after a ....(15) of caring for others.

School	conditions	hospital	days	money
group	medals	woman	patients	lamp
life	childhood	officers	illness	Britain

Space

Space continues in all directions, with no known limits, ...(1) infinity. It is

the empty area which all objects ....(2) the universe move within. All planets,

stars and galaxies ....(3) minute compared to the vast openness of space.

The ....(4) is surrounded by air. This air is the atmosphere ....(5)

protects our planet from space. The further from Earth ....(6) go, the thinner

the air becomes. The air runs ....(7) at about 95 kilometres from the Earth's

surface. This ....(8) where space begins. Outer space, or beyond the

atmosphere, ...(9) not entirely empty. It contains dust, meteoroids and even

..............................(10) of spacecraft that have been launched from Earth.

The ....(11) between planets in our Solar System is called 'interplanetary

..............................'(12). The Sun's gravity controls the movement of planets in

..............................(13) space to form orbits. Distances in 'interplanetary space' are

..............................(14) in millions of kilometres. For example, the distance between

..............................(15) Earth and the Sun is 150 million kilometres.

The ....(16) between the stars is called 'interstellar space'. The distances

..............................(17) 'interstellar space' are measured in light years. This is

..............................(18) distance light travels in one year. The nearest star

..............................(19) the Sun is Proxima Centauri, which is nearly 4.5 ....(20)

years (45 trillion kilometres) from the Sun.

Beyond this ....(21) is 'intergalactic space'. That is, the space between

galaxies, ...(22) distance so vast it reaches almost beyond our imaginations!

light	to	Earth	thousands	the	
is	from	that	out	in	to
space	are	this	is	measured	space
a	space	you	space	the	

Salinity

Use the following words to complete the passage.
You will need to use the map to complete some of the answers.

drainage	Brazil	salts	occurs	Colorado	China	areas
Tigris	Ethiopia	years	available	problem	remove	volunteers	Egypt
watertable		vegetation		Victoria		Indonesia	notice

Salt ....(1) naturally in soil and poses no ....(2) until

people upset nature's balance. Thousands of

..................................(3) ago the Sumerians salinated

the soil near the Euphrates and ....(4)

rivers by inappropriate agricultural practices.

Clearing deep-rooted native ....(5)

to grow shallow-rooted crops which don't

use all the ....(6) ground water,

causes the watertable to rise. This brings soluble

..................................(7) closer to the surface, which

in turn inhibit plant growth. ....(8) in South America, Australia and near

neighbour ....(9), are still clearing huge ....(10) of natural

vegetation. In Australia, ...(11) plant millions of trees, and deep drains and

aquifer pumps are also used to ....(12) excess groundwater.

Overuse of irrigation water also raises the ....(13) especially in areas with

poor ....(14). Salinity is slow and silent; it may be 25 years before farmers

..................................(15) that their trees are dying.

Salt eventually kills plants.

Salty water.

Watertable rises.

Millions of hectares worldwide are affected: the state of

..................................(16) in the USA; salt crusts on farmland in

..................................(17), the Sudan and ....(18)

on the African continent; problems near the Yellow River in

..................................(19); and Western Australia and the states of

NSW and ....(20) in Australia have problems.

Colorado *Tigris* *Yellow River* *Egypt* *Euphrates* *Sudan* *Ethiopia* *Brazil* *Indonesia* *Western Australia* *NSW* *Victoria*

Areas of severe salinity

Oliver Twist

England's great novelist Charles Dickens ....(1)

'Oliver Twist', a story of life in 19th century London slums.

It's about a boy whose mother ....(2) in

a workhouse for the poor after giving birth to Oliver. At

nine he ....(3) work at another children's

workhouse. Because he worked hard he was hungry so he

...........................(4) more food and for his impudence he was

...........................(5). He was also badly treated by another

young worker.

Later, Oliver ran away to London. There he ....(6) Jack Dawkins, the

'Artful Dodger', who ....(7) him to Fagin, a cruel old man who had

...........................(8) a gang of young pickpockets. Soon he left Fagin's

house but Bill Sykes and his girlfriend Nancy, Fagin's friends,

...........................(9) him to go back.

Eventually Oliver ....(10) that Sykes had killed

Nancy and some time later had accidentally ....(11)

himself. Fagin had been ....(12) to be hanged

and Jack ....(13) for his crimes. Oliver was

...........................(14) by the kind, rich Mr Brownlow and they

lived happily in a small country village.

Dickens wrote his novel to bring attention to the wretched lives

...........................(15) by poor people in the workhouses and slum

areas of London.

requested	dies	adopted	sentenced	heard
led	organised	met	began	imprisoned
hanged	forced	wrote	introduced	punished

Big Book of Cloze – Upper

Acid Rain

Use the following phrases to complete the passage.
Phrases are groups of words which don't make complete sense by themselves.
Each adverb phrase (of place) answers the question, 'Where?'.

- *inside homes*
- *around the world*
- *in the northern hemisphere*
- *in power plants*
- *in nearby Germany*
- *around the local district*
- *in the US Congress*

- *on monuments*
- *in scientific records*
- *in many waterways*
- *to affected water*
- *in fish populations*
- *in Asia*   • *in Europe*
- *in snow*   • *from fuels*

- *from volcanoes*
- *through the air*
- *in the water*
- *in England*

The name 'acid rain' results from early atmospheric studies

....[1]. Sulphuric and nitric acids are found

in acid rain and ....[2]. Fossil fuels, oil and

coal, burnt in factories and ....[3],

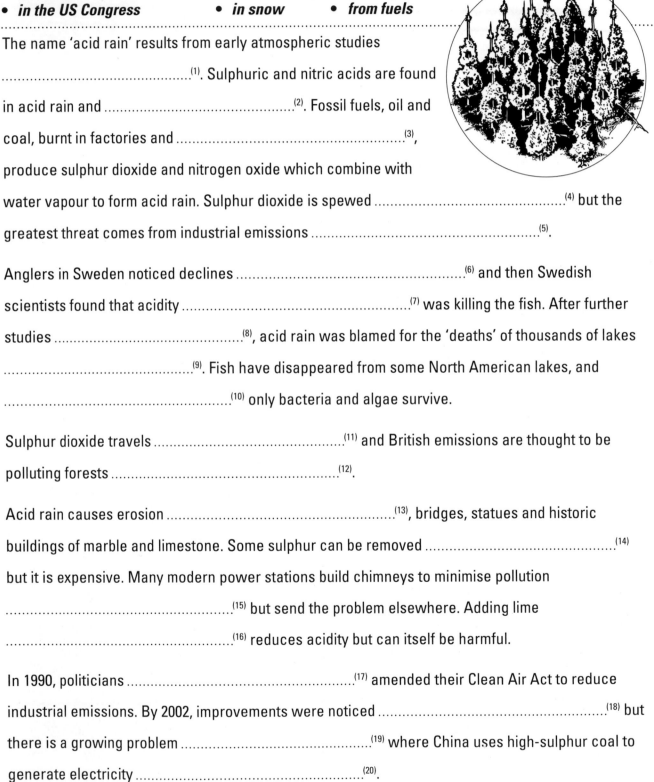

produce sulphur dioxide and nitrogen oxide which combine with

water vapour to form acid rain. Sulphur dioxide is spewed ....[4] but the

greatest threat comes from industrial emissions ....[5].

Anglers in Sweden noticed declines ....[6] and then Swedish

scientists found that acidity ....[7] was killing the fish. After further

studies ....[8], acid rain was blamed for the 'deaths' of thousands of lakes

....[9]. Fish have disappeared from some North American lakes, and

....[10] only bacteria and algae survive.

Sulphur dioxide travels ....[11] and British emissions are thought to be

polluting forests ....[12].

Acid rain causes erosion ....[13], bridges, statues and historic

buildings of marble and limestone. Some sulphur can be removed ....[14]

but it is expensive. Many modern power stations build chimneys to minimise pollution

....[15] but send the problem elsewhere. Adding lime

....[16] reduces acidity but can itself be harmful.

In 1990, politicians ....[17] amended their Clean Air Act to reduce

industrial emissions. By 2002, improvements were noticed ....[18] but

there is a growing problem ....[19] where China uses high-sulphur coal to

generate electricity ....[20].

Spacecraft

People who build spacecrafts do so in special factories. ....(1) factories need to be very clean as the slightest ....(2) of dust or dirt might later cause major problems.

................................(3) parts of the spacecraft are tested many times before ....(4) launched into space.

The biggest problem for any spacecraft ....(5) getting into space. The Earth's pull, or gravity, is ....(6) strong so spacecraft must have rockets fitted to them ....(7) help them get into space. To reach space the ....(8) need to make the spacecraft attain a speed of ....(9) kilometres per second. This speed is called the 'orbital ....'(10) and happens 190 kilometres above the Earth's surface. The ....(11) can now freely orbit the Earth. However, if the ....(12) is headed for further destinations, such as the Moon, ...(13) speed needs to increase to 12 kilometres per second. ....(14) speed is called 'escape velocity' and means the spacecraft ....(15) broken away from the Earth's pull, or gravity.

To ....(16) further again, for example to another planet such as ....(17) , the spacecraft must be launched from Earth at a ....(18) (speed direction) greater than the 'escape velocity'. The craft ....(19) then go into 'solar orbit' to carry it to ....(20) target planet. The 'Viking' space probe has sent back ....(21) information from orbiting and landing on Mars.

its	bit	velocity	to	spacecraft	travel	All
spacecraft	being	is	rockets	This	Mars	would
These	valuable	very	eight	has	velocity	the

Genetically Modified (GM) Foods

Use the following words to complete the passage.

engineered	heart	extra	bees	starving	grown	donated
tomatoes	protests	Australia	dangerous	insect	Canada	milk
tastier	resistant	seeds	size	concern		supermarkets

Lactic acid added to foods prevents ....(1) bacteria developing, and fish oil added to milk can reduce ....(2) disease. People accept these 'value-added foods', but GM foods still cause ....(3) about long-term health effects so they need to be labelled in ....(4). Low-cholesterol margarine is made from canola ....(5), but now GM canola is produced in America and its neighbour ....(6), while crops like wheat are being trialled in ....(7). One problem is that GM pollen carried by winds or ....(8) could affect nearby crops.

Fifty-three million hectares of GM crops were ....(9) worldwide in 2002. They are similar to normal crops but possess an ....(10) gene inserted by DNA technology; e.g. a gene that protects them from ....(11) pests. Genes can also be removed and a gene which caused ....(12) in California to break down was removed so ....(13) tomatoes were then produced. A dahlia gene inserted into bananas will make them ....(14) to the fungal disease siggatoka and an extra gene makes cows' ....(15) more nutritious. GM salmon now grow to full ....(16) in a quarter of the time after being ....(17) with another fish's gene.

In 2002, Zambia discovered that the free maize ....(18) by America was genetically engineered. Zambia's government then banned it, even though 3 000 000 Zambians were ....(19)! The European Union, where ....(20) first started in Germany, also banned GM foods in the same year. It appears that the concerns are still present.

Easter

Easter is the ....(1) of the Christian festivals and remembers the death of Jesus on a ....(2) cross on Good Friday and his resurrection on Easter Sunday.

In many northern countries ancient tribes thought the heathen goddess Eostre brought the world to life in the ....(3) Spring with new flowers, fresh green leaves, etc. As Jesus was also given new life, some experts believe the ....(4) Christians adopted her name.

The Ancient Greeks and Romans ate ....(5) bread with crosses on at many festivals. Christians began to use the symbol on ....(6) cross buns to remind them of how Jesus had died. The Ancient Egyptians believed the ....(7) rabbit was a sign of new life in Spring, perhaps because it had so many babies. Over 200 years ago ....(8) migrant children took the custom of making ....(9) nests for their 'Easter Hare' to America, where it became the 'Easter Bunny'.

Eggs are also a sign of ....(10) life. In China and Persia 3000 years ago eggs were coloured red or decorated. In ....(11) Europe women and children spend hours drawing ....(12) designs on Easter eggs using wax and ....(13) dyes. For over 100 years an annual egg-rolling event for ....(14) children twelve and under has been held on the ....(15) lawns of the White House, home of the US President.

ordinary	new	modern	attractive	early
green	oldest	young	wooden	coloured
warm	German	baked	hot	cosy

Forensic Science

Use the following words to complete the passage.

criminal	successfully	phones	types	others	fluids	hair
analyse	police	cells	now	stream	sift	comparison
clearly	weapon	voluntarily	identify	programs		traced

Technology in forensic science is helping

.............................(1) forces to fight criminals

more ....(2) and Melbourne

University has the world's first forensic medicine

centre. Modern tools include: computer

.................................(3) that change fuzzy

surveillance tapes into ....(4)-seen

images; infra-red spectrometers which identify

different.................................(5) of ink used on

ransom demands; ....(6)

microscopes to scientifically compare bullets; chemical scanners that ....(7)

evidence and very controversial sensors which ....(8) a suspect's brainwaves.

Crime investigators can use electron microscopes to send a ....(9) of

electrons on to material recently handled by a ....(10) so that, for example, any

gunpowder from a ....(11) the suspect is accused of using can be identified.

We ....(12) know that voiceprints from secretly tapped ....(13)

are unique, like DNA and fingerprints, and can be ....(14) to an individual.

DNA cells are extracted from ....(15) like sweat, tears and saliva, or from

body tissues, in order to ....(16) a particular person. DNA is only found in

.................................(17) with a nucleus, so cells from teeth, fingernails and

.................................(18) are ruled out. Many prisoners have refused to

.................................(19) give up their DNA, but DNA samples have cleared

.................................(20) already serving sentences in prisons. Nevertheless, these technologies

raise serious questions about rights to privacy.

Electron microscope

Deserts

There are two kinds of deserts, ...(1), both are dry. The few people living in or near deserts are often nomads seeking pasture ....(2) or oases, where water is regularly available, just as their ancestors have done ....(3).

Desert rainfall is unreliable and droughts can last ....(4). Temperatures often reach 40°C during the day but can plunge to freezing ....(5) under clear skies. Insects bring sandfly fever, the eye disease trachoma spread ....(6) and malaria from mosquitoes which breed ....(7). The hot sun bakes the ground dry, then dust storms blow away the valuable topsoil used to grow food ....(8) of deserts.

....(9), particularly by goats, the destruction ....(10) and poor farming methods some desert regions are spreading, so scientists have to work harder to improve the situation. ....(11), like Algeria and Saudi Arabia, scientists have reduced areas of desert. They pumped in water ....(12) using solar-powered water pumps, and enriched the soil together with improved farming methods. These improvements have led to increases ....(13). Unfortunately, the wealth obtained from the sale of new crops ....(14) has not reached the ordinary desert people, who still live ....(15) in this harsh environment.

- *in the oases*
- *for their animals*
- *in some desert populations*
- *for centuries*
- *in poverty*
- *by flies*
- *over long distances*
- *at night*
- *In richer countries*
- *for years*
- *like cotton*
- *hot or cold*
- *of trees*
- *on the edges*
- *Because of overgrazing*

The Laser (Light Amplification by Stimulated Emission of Radiation)

Use the following nouns to complete the passage.

research	time	operations	music	enemies	relics	millimetre
beams	vessels	films	computer		target	colours
light	surgeons	mixture	warriors	colour	infection	point

Lasers are concentrated ....(1) of monochromatic light on the same narrow wavelength. They are one pure ....(2), whereas normal light is a ....(3) of lightwaves. A laser beam can be concentrated to a ....(4) less than one micron, a thousandth of a ....(5).

Space ....(6) produced a working laser in the 1960s and now they reproduce ....(7) from compact discs and are used in supermarket barcode scanners. Excimer lasers used in delicate medical ....(8) do not burn surrounding tissues and are used to seal leaking blood ....(9)—even those in the eyes—or clear clogged arteries. Many ....(10) prefer lasers to scalpels as there is less chance of ....(11) or bleeding.

In missiles, a laser beam illuminates a ....(12) and the missile's detectors home in on the reflected beam of ....(13). Such 21st century military developments were even suggested in early ....(14), such as when James Bond was threatened with death beams by his ....(15) in Goldfinger!

Surveyors can aim lasers at distant buildings with a ....(16) calculating the distance from the ....(17) taken for the light to return. Scientists are excited about the possible use of lasers to restore the faded ....(18) of the 6000 fragile Chinese terracotta ....(19) of Xian without damaging these priceless ....(20) from the past.

People in Space

The first spacecraft was launched by the Soviet Union ....(1) 4 October 1957. It was called *Sputnik 1*. This ....(2) began the space age. The first human in space ....(3) Soviet cosmomaut Yuri Gagarin. The flight in which he ....(4) the Earth was made on the 12 April 1961 ....(5) his spacecraft *Vostok 1*. On 20 February 1962, John ....(6) became the first American to orbit the Earth. Since ....(7) early times many thousands of spacecraft have been launched. ....(8) next target was the Moon. *Apollo 8* astronauts orbited ....(9) Moon ten times in December 1968. Then, on 20 ....(10) 1969, Neil Armstrong and Edwin Aldrin became the first ....(11) to step onto the Moon. Further explorations saw the ....(12) of the first space shuttle in April 1981. This ....(13) the first manned spacecraft designed to be reused.

When ....(14) go into space they must be protected because space ....(15) no air and the temperatures can be very hot ....(16) very cold. Spacecraft and space suits must provide people ....(17) this protection. They must also allow people to breathe, ...(18), drink, sleep and keep clean. Food and drink on ....(19) spacecraft must be easy to prepare and healthy. To ....(20) clean, astronauts bathe with wet towels. When they sleep ....(21) use special sleeping bags which strap them to a ....(22) surface and their pillow. This stops them floating and ....(23) around the cabin while they are asleep.

Astronauts' space ....(24) provide a life support system for when they venture ....(25) the spacecraft.

on	*Glenn*	*humans*	*or*	*they*
event	*these*	*launch*	*with*	*soft*
was	*Scientists'*	*was*	*eat*	*bouncing*
orbited	*the*	*people*	*a*	*suits*
aboard	*July*	*has*	*keep*	*outside*

Cloning

Use the following adverbs to complete the passage.
They are either adverbs of time (e.g. soon, often) or manner (e.g. carefully).

successfully	definitely	passionately	regularly	sometimes	recently
chemically	angrily	expertly	generously	happily	then	wisely
now	carefully	openly	steadily	again	solely	often

Dolly the sheep was ....(1) cloned in 1997 and CC (Carbon Copy), the cat,

in Texas in 2002. Since then, scientists have ....(2) discussed the

possible side-effects of human cloning. Korean researchers ....(3) claimed to

have cloned a human embryo but several countries have ....(4) halted such

experiments, though a cloned baby was reportedly born in Italy in 2003. US President, George

W Bush, once said he was most ....(5) 100% opposed to human cloning.

Scientists answer any criticisms ....(6) by claiming they want to use stem

cells ....(7) for the problems of disease, injury and old age.

In cloning, the nucleus of a cell from a patient is ....(8) extracted. It is

implanted into a donor's denucleated egg cell and ....(9) treated. The

embryo soon grows as the cells divide and multiply ....(10). The cloned

cells can ....(11) be implanted into the patient ....(12). In

experiments so far, the embryos haven't developed far enough for stem cells to be extracted

..............................(13).

Scientists have ....(14) obtained stem

cells from cloned mouse embryos. However, human

experiments are an unpleasant, expensive, and

..............................(15) dangerous procedure for those

women who ....(16) donate eggs. To obtain

eggs ....(17), one American cell technology

company has ....(18) offered donors

payments and many have ....(19) accepted. Of course, millions of natural

clones ....(20) roam the Earth—except we call them identical twins!

Earthquakes

The surface of the Earth is made up of ....(1) like those on an onion. We live on the crust which ....(2) on a deep layer called a mantle. The mantle is almost 3000 km thick and is mostly hot ....(3) rock formed by the intense heat inside the ....(4). Many scientists believe the crust is ....(5) up into tectonic plates with cracks around their edges. ....(6) mostly occur along these fault lines when plates ....(7) as they float on the mantle. Sometimes, following a major shock, there are several ....(8) tremors called aftershocks. A strong undersea earthquake can cause ....(9) waves called tsunamis to sweep ashore and ....(10) thousands of people. Severe damage is usual at the ....(11), the surface area directly above the earthquake.

Some great cities have been ....(12) by earthquakes with great loss of life as in Tokyo in 1923. In China in 1556 an ....(13) 830 000 people died and in 1976 many more thousands lost their lives.

Improved building designs mean some modern skyscrapers can visibly ....(14) but not be damaged because of the materials used in their ....(15).

estimated	collide	Earthquakes	devastated	drown
liquid	sway	epicentre	Earth	giant
construction	floats	layers	smaller	broken

The Future in Space

Scientists are planning to put a base on the ....(1) within the next decade.

A lot of people ....(2) a Moon base is an important step towards exploring

.............................(3) rest of the Solar System and perhaps creating a ....(4)

on Mars. Scientists also believe that the Moon could ....(5) such things as

oxygen or metals.

The next great ....(6) forward will be sending people to Mars. If such

.............................(7) trip happens it will take the astronauts a ....(8) to get to

Mars and a year to return. The ....(9) that would carry these astronauts

would have to be ....(10) enough to carry all the fuel, food, water

and ....(11) supplies, plus give the astronauts a comfortable place

to ....(12) , for the entire journey. Once near Mars the spacecraft

.............................(13) need to orbit the planet. Perhaps a smaller craft ....(14)

then be sent down to the surface of the ....(15). People could walk on the

planet and gather samples ....(16) the soil and rocks and later take off to

.............................(17) to the main ship for the return trip to Earth.

.............................(18) space stretching

so far into endless unknowns, the future

.............................(19) space travel

and discoveries is limited only by our

.............................(20) technology. Who knows

what lies ahead for future generations;

.............................(21) living in space and

travelling freely between planets and

.............................(22) is closer than we think.

Moon	spacecraft	perhaps	big	provide	year	believe		
With	planet	scientific	the	would	return	a		could
for	galaxies	live	base	step	other	of		

Animal to Human Transplants (Xenotransplantation)

Use the following words to complete the passage.

dangers	measles	chemicals	died	inserted	bodies	rejected
opposed	deadly	sick	outside	serious	common	groups
available	Africa	centres	drugs	differences		attack

On the ....(1) of human cells are 'marker chemicals' (proteins). If animal cells are put into our ....(2) they are seen as foreign, so our white blood cells ....(3) them. With organ transplants this is called 'rejection' and ....(4) are needed to control it, often with ....(5) side-effects. There are too few human heart donors so genetic engineering scientists have ....(6) human genes into fertilised pig eggs. When each pig matures it has a heart with human marker ....(7). Though patients may die from other causes the scientists believe these hearts would not be ....(8) and could be used until human hearts are ....(9). This could save thousands, perhaps millions, of ....(10) patients worldwide.

As diseases like HIV, flu and ....(11) appear to have come from animals, there is the risk that a ....(12) animal retrovirus could cross to humans, like the dreaded Ebola virus in ....(13). Already there are patients who have ....(14) shortly after animal organ transplants and critics claim it will be at least a decade before the ....(15) are fully realised.

Many church and animal protection ....(16) are against further developments, so the location of English research ....(17) is secret. There are also cultural ....(18) to be faced. Organ transplants between even humans are generally unacceptable in Japan, but ....(19) in America and Europe, and some countries are totally ....(20) to xenotransplants! Perhaps encouraging more human donors is the answer.

Answers

The Lord of the Rings 1
1. language
2. voted
3. screen
4. Return
5. actors
6. director
7. landscapes
8. found
9. travelling
10. wizard
11. companions
12. destroying
13. journey
14. forces
15. regain
16. creation
17. might
18. again
19. struggle
20. twists

Edward Jenner 2
1. by a virus
2. in the air
3. for life
4. centuries ago
5. In some wars
6. to North America
7. with liquid
8. A British doctor
9. from smallpox
10. a mild cattle disease
11. from a dairymaid's sore
12. on the boy
13. In 1967
14. in a laboratory

Changing Art 3
1. tombs
2. heroes
3. Romans
4. centuries
5. people
6. museums
7. insurance
8. paintings
9. world
10. film
11. government
12. example
13. paint
14. surface
15. money
16. University
17. lovers
18. complaints
19. room
20. elephants

The Milky Way 4
1. of
2. groups
3. Milky
4. the
5. stars
6. bulge
7. arms
8. The
9. Solar
10. those
11. its
12. orbit
13. galaxy
14. galaxy
15. bulge
16. known
17. of
18. are
19. everything
20. distances
21. year
22. galaxy
23. at
24. distances

Child Stars 5
1. famous
2. first
3. successful/popular
4. little
5. humorous
6. youngest
7. British
8. paltry
9. sensible
10. American
11. popular/successful
12. endless
13. annual
14. financial

15. young
16. bitter
17. cheating
18. troubled
19. finest
20. normal

Hercules 6
1. Roman
2. strong
3. hated
4. cradle
5. young
6. music
7. madness
8. serve
9. Hydra
10. arrows
11. descended
12. guarding
13. search
14. carried
15. daughter

The Family Car 7
1. airbags
2. important
3. experimenting
4. suffers/has
5. safe/specific
6. researched
7. developed
8. message
9. shake/vibrate
10. expensive
11. manufactured
12. mixed
13. eventually
14. agreed/begun
15. engines/motors
16. vehicle/car
17. empty
18. view
19. combine
20. companies

The Romans 8
1. brother
2. messenger
3. Christians
4. races
5. warriors
6. ruins
7. countries
8. catapults
9. cities
10. roads
11. Britain
12. emperor
13. schools
14. slaves
15. education

Transport in the Future 9
1. differ
2. true
3. moving
4. personal
5. Olympics
6. air
7. private
8. huge
9. called
10. metres
11. down
12. engines
13. weight
14. airports
15. roof
16. litres
17. up
18. deafening
19. cheaper
20. built

The Solar System 10
1. is
2. Solar
3. a
4. travel
5. moons
6. centre
7. times
8. put
9. the
10. over
11. planets
12. Sun
13. and
14. the
15. rock
16. a
17. Jupiter
18. left-over
19. of
20. are
21. tail
22. or

Mobile Phones 11
1. palm
2. digital
3. moving
4. using
5. Net/Internet
6. read/interpret
7. pay
8. current

9. form
10. mobile
11. numbers
12. late
13. characters
14. language
15. messages
16. health
17. warned
18. teenagers
19. parents
20. teachers

Communications History 12
1. different
2. earliest
3. flat
4. long
5. dense
6. carved
7. coloured
8. short
9. polished
10. worldwide
11. modern
12. human
13. electrical
14. glass
15. original

The Sun 13
1. our
2. glowing
3. All
4. appears
5. the
6. million
7. eight
8. nearest
9. a
10. than
11. made
12. the
13. million
14. in
15. it
16. to
17. the
18. Without
19. Plants
20. a
21. the
22. out
23. light
24. of

Bullying 14
1. aware
2. beware
3. names
4. games
5. tall
6. all
7. tease
8. ease
9. choose
10. lose
11. school
12. cruel
13. peers
14. tears
15. TV
16. see
17. rules
18. schools
19. outside
20. denied

Television 15
1. in the early years
2. a Scottish engineer
3. two years later
4. in his honour
5. from a scene
6. into electronic signals
7. at the same time
8. to a picture tube
9. by our aerials
10. back to the original pictures
11. through the air
12. over greater distances
13. to news items
14. within communities
15. by young people

Body Image 16
1. indicate/show
2. teachers
3. better
4. apparent/seen
5. ugly
6. beautiful/slim
7. impossible
8. lead
9. dangerous
10. loss
11. two/some
12. school

Answers

13. lose
14. said
15. appearance
16. self/body
17. them/children
18. culture
19. around
20. considered

Mercury 17
1. is
2. to
3. it
4. a
5. orbit
6. Romans
7. gods
8. It
9. once
10. the
11. a
12. Earth
13. that
14. and
15. formed
16. very
17. on
18. hot
19. of
20. be
21. side
22. can
23. None
24. survive
25. lack

Limited Overs Cricket 18
1. played
2. matches
3. main
4. involved
5. popular
6. part
7. players
8. millions
9. form
10. International
11. colourful
12. critics
13. supporters
14. result
15. different
16. slips
17. third
18. Apart
19. gully
20. three

Dinosaurs 19
1. terrible
2. studying
3. ground
4. footprints
5. protection
6. huge
7. wife
8. collected
9. world
10. cleaned
11. plastic
12. disappeared
13. clouds
14. plants
15. ate

Extreme Sports 20
1. Extreme
2. physical
3. individual
4. obvious
5. greatest
6. various
7. high-rise
8. dangerous
9. in-line
10. every
11. broken
12. long
13. important
14. firm
15. serious
16. several
17. artificial
18. increasing
19. particular
20. local

Neptune 21
1. myths
2. power
3. storms
4. wine
5. people
6. lives
7. times
8. Saturn
9. fish
10. spear
11. fishermen
12. whip
13. fountains
14. Rome
15. moon

Recycling 22
1. paper
2. cartons
3. reduces
4. household

5. required
6. regulations
7. food
8. lifted
9. roads
10. recycled
11. bacteria
12. drunk
13. washes
14. fires
15. supplies
16. technology
17. Europe
18. small
19. find
20. expensive

The Moon 23
1. Although
2. sky
3. moonlight
4. If
5. the
6. the
7. gravity
8. 60 kg
9. Even
10. each
11. other
12. with
13. no
14. is
15. formed
16. surface
17. plains
18. is
19. space
20. be
21. first
22. one
23. landed
24. expeditions
25. more

Robots 24
1. led
2. are
3. produced
4. walked
5. assemble
6. weld
7. programmed
8. approach
9. Equipped
10. searched
11. destroyed
12. driven
13. interacts
14. recognises
15. understand
16. reacts
17. mow
18. find
19. distinguish
20. solve

The Tiger 25
1. wild
2. entire
3. ten
4. magnificent
5. Asian
6. poor
7. young
8. aching
9. painful
10. striped
11. cruel
12. valuable
13. profitable
14. recent
15. tropical

Comets 26
1. System
2. a
3. surrounds
4. nucleus
5. centre
6. ball
7. kilometres
8. and
9. dioxide
10. close
11. and
12. and
13. Sun
14. streak
15. of
16. ice
17. turn
18. Earth
19. and
20. seen
21. close
22. telescope
23. comets
24. Comet
25. predicted
26. that
27. years
28. beyond
29. in

High-speed Trains 27
1. design
2. steel
3. cables
4. magnetic
5. reached
6. above
7. magnets
8. currents
9. train
10. waves
11. attraction
12. Airport

13. expensive
14. expected
15. England
16. contact
17. silent
18. maintenance
19. power
20. environment

The Motor Car 28
1. driven
2. developed
3. gain
4. explodes
5. recharged
6. passed
7. warn
8. built
9. stood
10. added
11. replaced
12. made
13. shatter
14. breathe
15. kill

Exploring the Ocean
Depths 29
1. major
2. possible
3. marine
4. useful
5. enormous
6. normal
7. several
8. terrible
9. electric
10. similar
11. American
12. sophisticated
13. amazing
14. popular
15. recent
16. unknown
17. industrial
18. toxic
19. upper
20. lifeless

Meteors 30
1. seen
2. shooting
3. when
4. enters
5. Air
6. hot
7. lasts
8. actually
9. they
10. of
11. ever
12. and
13. at
14. types
15. rock
16. of
17. may
18. weigh
19. substantial
20. small
21. surface
22. the
23. thought
24. that
25. meteorites
26. preserved

Protecting Our Borders ... 31
1. always
2. secretly
3. strictly
4. often
5. cruelly
6. easily
7. recently
8. unsuccessfully
9. obviously
10. adequately
11. heavily
12. given
13. badly
14. foolishly
15. horrifyingly
16. gradually
17. specially
18. now
19. Fortunately
20. almost

The First Fleet 32
1. first
2. miserable
3. leaky
4. terrible
5. damp
6. welcome
7. fresh
8. violent
9. suitable
10. scarce
11. new
12. dangerous
13. magnificent
14. deep
15. east

Answers

Global Warming 33
1. emissions
2. temperature
3. support
4. rise
5. populations
6. changes
7. countries
8. India
9. responsible
10. graph
11. thirty-six
12. Japan
13. Canada
14. trees
15. annually
16. earnt
17. paying
18. America
19. country
20. aim

Spring 34
1. time
2. green
3. gather
4. where
5. shorter
6. players
7. hot
8. colourful
9. broken
10. washing
11. dawns
12. happy
13. smooth
14. lambs
15. butterflies

Tectonic Plates – Earthquakes 35
1. millions
2. thick
3. Earth
4. float
5. forced
6. pressures
7. Black
8. north
9. next
10. slowly
11. south
12. illegal
13. buildings
14. damage
15. cartoons
16. safety
17. earthquake
18. Turkey
19. Peru
20. China

Asteroids 36
1. the
2. Sometimes
3. be
4. up
5. together
6. in
7. Thousands
8. Ceres
9. to
10. in
11. Most
12. six
13. while
14. combined
15. Moon
16. the
17. may
18. Hermes
19. a
20. the
21. major
22. extinction

Water is Precious 37
1. found
2. lies
3. predicts
4. performed
5. attempted
6. turn
7. provide
8. survive
9. water
10. depend
11. import
12. opened
13. producing
14. possessed
15. put
16. want
17. help
18. soak
19. fix
20. collect

Florence Nightingale 38
1. childhood
2. days
3. group
4. Britain
5. hospital

6. conditions
7. patients
8. lamp
9. officers
10. medals
11. money
12. School
13. illness
14. woman
15. life

Space 39
1. to
2. from
3. are
4. Earth
5. that
6. you
7. out
8. is
9. is
10. thousands
11. space
12. space
13. this
14. measured
15. the
16. space
17. in
18. the
19. to
20. light
21. space
22. a

Salinity 40
1. occurs
2. problem
3. years
4. Tigris
5. vegetation
6. available
7. salts
8. Brazil
9. Indonesia
10. areas
11. volunteers
12. remove
13. watertable
14. drainage
15. notice
16. Colorado
17. Egypt/Ethiopia
18. Ethiopia/Egypt
19. China
20. Victoria

Oliver Twist 41
1. wrote
2. dies
3. began
4. requested
5. punished
6. met
7. introduced
8. organised
9. forced
10. heard
11. hanged
12. sentenced
13. imprisoned
14. adopted
15. led

Acid Rain 42
1. in England
2. in snow
3. inside homes
4. from volcanoes
5. in the northern hemisphere
6. in fish populations
7. in the water
8. around the world
9. in Europe
10. in many waterways
11. through the air
12. in nearby Germany
13. on monuments
14. from fuels
15. around the local district
16. to affected water
17. in the US Congress
18. in scientific records
19. in Asia
20. in power plants

Spacecraft 43
1. These
2. bit
3. All
4. being
5. is
6. very
7. to
8. rockets
9. eight
10. velocity
11. spacecraft
12. spacecraft
13. its
14. This
15. has
16. travel
17. Mars
18. velocity
19. would
20. the
21. valuable

Genetically Modified GM Foods 44
1. dangerous
2. heart
3. concern
4. supermarkets
5. seeds
6. Canada
7. Australia
8. bees
9. grown
10. extra
11. insect
12. tomatoes
13. tastier
14. resistant
15. milk
16. size
17. engineered
18. donated
19. starving
20. protests

Easter 45
1. oldest
2. wooden
3. warm
4. early
5. baked
6. hot
7. ordinary
8. German
9. cosy
10. new
11. modern
12. attractive
13. coloured
14. young
15. green

Forensic Science 46
1. police
2. successfully
3. programs
4. clearly
5. types
6. comparison
7. sift
8. analyse
9. stream
10. criminal
11. weapon
12. now
13. phones
14. traced
15. fluids
16. identify
17. cells
18. hair
19. voluntarily
20. others

Deserts 47
1. hot or cold
2. for their animals
3. for centuries
4. for years
5. at night
6. by flies
7. in the oases
8. on the edges
9. Because of over grazing
10. of trees
11. In richer countries
12. over long distances
13. in some desert populations
14. like cotton
15. in poverty

Answers

The Laser 48

1. beams	2. colour	3. mixture
4. point	5. millimetre	6. research
7. music	8. operations	9. vessels
10. surgeons	11. infection	12. target
13. light	14. films	15. enemies
16. computer	17. time	18. colours
19. warriors	20. relics	

People in Space 49

1. on	2. event	3. was
4. orbited	5. aboard	6. Glenn
7. these	8. Scientists'	9. the
10. July	11. humans	12. launch
13. was	14. people	15. has
16. or	17. with	18. eat
19. a	20. keep	21. they
22. soft	23. bouncing	24. suits
25. outside		

Cloning 50

1. expertly	2. passionately
3. recently	4. wisely
5. definitely	6. angrily
7. solely	8. carefully
9. chemically	10. steadily
11. then	12. again
13. successfully	14. often
15. sometimes	16. generously
17. regularly	18. openly
19. happily	20. now

Earthquakes 51

1. layers	2. floats
3. liquid	4. Earth
5. broken	6. Earthquakes
7. collide	8. smaller
9. giant	10. drown
11. epicentre	12. devastated
13. estimated	14. sway
15. construction	

The Future in Space 52

1. Moon	2. believe	3. the
4. base	5. provide	6. step
7. a	8. year	9. spacecraft
10. big	11. other	12. live
13. would	14. could	15. planet
16. of	17. return	18. With
19. for	20. scientific	21. perhaps
22. galaxies		

Animal to Human Transplants 53

1. outside	2. bodies
3. attack	4. drugs
5. serious	6. inserted
7. chemicals	8. rejected

9. available	10. sick
11. measles	12. deadly
13. Africa	14. died
15. dangers	16. groups
17. centres	18. differences
19. common	20. opposed